Favourite Australian Poems

Illustrated by

Ron Driscoll

CHILD & ASSOCIATES
AN ALL-AUSTRALIAN PUBLISHER

Published by
Child and Associates Publishing Pty Ltd,
9 Clearview Place, Brookvale, NSW, Australia, 2100
A wholly owned Australian publishing company
This book has been edited, designed and typeset
in Australia by the Publisher

First Edition 1987

Typesetting processed by Deblaere and Associates
Printed in Singapore by Kyodo Shing Loong Pty Ltd

National Library of Australia
Cataloguing-in-Publication

ISBN 0 86777 052 X.
I. Australian poetry. I. Driscoll, Ron.

A823'.008

The Publishers gratefully acknowledge Angus & Robertson Publishers and the copyright holders for permission to reprint the following poems: 'The Willows' (*Poems,* James Devaney, © Kevin Thompson 1950), 'Clancy of the Overflow' (*The Collected Verse of A. B. Paterson,* A. B. Paterson, © Retusa Pty Ltd 1921), 'The Crane Is My Neighbour' (*The Poems of Shaw Neilson,* John Shaw Neilson, © John McKimm 1965), Extract 'Swans at Night' (*Selected Verse,* Mary Gilmore, © Estate late Dame Mary Gilmore 1948), 'A Morning Song' and 'West' (*Selected Verse of C. J. Dennis,* C. J. Dennis, © Angus & Robertson Ltd 1950), and 'Calling to Me' *(Around the Boree Log,* John O'Brien, © F. A. Mecham1921).

Contents

HENRY LAWSON

The Blue Mountains

Above the ashes straight and tall,
  Through ferns with moisture dripping,
I climb beneath the sandstone wall,
  My feet on mosses slipping.

Like ramparts round the valley's edge
  The tinted cliffs are standing.
With many a broken wall and ledge,
  And many a rocky landing.

And round about their rugged feet
  Deep ferny dells are hidden
In shadowed depths, whence dust and heat
  Are banished and forbidden.

The stream that, crooning to itself,
  Comes down a tireless rover,
Flows calmly to the rocky shelf,
  And there leaps bravely over.

Now pouring down, now lost in spray
  When mountain breezes sally,
The water strikes the rock midway,
  And leaps into the valley.

Now in the west the colours change,
  The blue with crimson blending;
Behind the far Dividing Range,
  The sun is fast descending.

And mellowed day comes o'er the place,
  And softens ragged edges;
The rising moon's great placid face
  Looks gravely o'er the ledges.

Ron Driscoll
1987.

HENRY KENDALL

Bell-birds

By channels of coolness the echoes are calling,
And down the dim gorges I hear the creek falling;
It lives in the mountain, where moss and the sedges
Touch with their beauty the banks and the ledges;
Through brakes of the cedar and sycamore bowers
Struggles the light that is love to the flowers.
And, softer than slumber, and sweeter than singing,
The notes of the bell-birds are running and ringing.

The silver-voiced bell-birds, the darlings of day-time,
They sing in September their songs of the May-time.
When shadows wax strong, and the thunder-bolts hurtle,
They hide with their fear in the leaves of the myrtle;
When rain and the sunbeams shine mingled together
They start up like fairies that follow fair weather,
And straightway the hues of their feathers unfolden
Are the green and the purple, the blue and the golden.

October, the maiden of bright yellow tresses,
Loiters for love in these cool wildernesses;
Loiters knee-deep in the grasses to listen,
Where dripping rocks gleam and the leafy pools glisten.
Then is the time when the water-moons splendid
Break with their gold, and are scattered or blended
Over the creeks, till the woodlands have warning
Of songs of the bell-bird and wings of the morning.

Ron Driscoll
1987

HENRY KENDALL

Welcome as waters unkissed by the summers
Are the voices of bell-birds to thirsty far-comers.
When fiery December sets foot in the forest,
And the need of the wayfarer presses the sorest,
Pent in the ridges for ever and ever,
The bell-birds direct him to spring and to river,
With ring and with ripple, like runnels whose torrents
Are toned by the pebbles and leaves in the currents.

Often I sit, looking back to a childhood
Mixt with the sights and the sounds of the wildwood,
Longing for power and the sweetness to fashion
Lyrics with beats like the heart-beats of passion—
Songs interwoven of lights and of laughters
Borrowed from bell-birds in far forest rafters;
So I might keep in the city and alleys
The beauty and strength of the deep mountain valleys,
Charming to slumber the pain of my losses
With glimpses of creeks and a vision of mosses.

—oOo—

Ron Driscoll
1987

C. J. DENNIS

A Morning Song

The thrush is in the wattle tree, an', "O, you pretty dear!"
He's callin' to his little wife for all the bush to hear.
  He's wantin' all the bush to know about his charmin' hen;
  He sings it over fifty times, an' then begins again.
For it's Mornin'! Mornin'! The world is wet with dew,
With tiny drops a-twinkle where the sun comes shinin' thro'.

The thrush is in the wattle tree, red robin's underneath,
The little blue-cap's dodgin' in an' out amongst the heath;
  An' they're singin', boy, they're singin' like they'd bust
    'emselves to bits;
  While up above, old Laughin' Jack is havin' forty fits.
For it's Mornin'! Mornin'! The leaves are all ashine:
There's treasure all about the place; an' all of it is mine.

Oh, it's good to be a wealthy man, it's grand to be a king
With mornin' on the forest-land an' joy in everything.
  It's fine to be a healthy man with healthy work to do
  In the singin' land, the clean land, washed again with dew.
When sunlight slants across the trees, an' birds begin to sing,
Then kings may snore in palaces, but I'm awake—and king.

But the king must cook his breakfast, an' the king must sweep
    the floor;
Then out with axe on shoulder to his kingdom at the door,
  His old dog sportin' on ahead, his troubles all behind,
  An' joy mixed in the blood of him because the world is kind.
For it's Mornin'! Mornin'! Time to out an' strive!
Oh, there's not a thing I'm askin' else but just to be alive!

Ron Driscoll
1987

My friends are in the underbrush, my friends are in the trees,
An' merrily they welcome me with mornin' melodies.
Above, below, from bush an' bough each calls his tuneful part;
An' best of all, one trusty friend is callin' in my heart.
For it's Mornin'! Mornin'! When night's black troubles end.
An' never man was friendless yet who stayed his own good friend.

Grey thrush is in the wattle, an' it's, "O, you pretty dear!"
He's callin' to his little wife, an' don't care who should hear
In the great bush, the fresh bush, washed again with dew;
An' my axe is on my shoulder, an' there's work ahead to do.
Oh, it's Mornin'! Singin' Mornin'! in the land I count the best,
An' with the heart an' mind of me I'm singin' with the rest.

—oOo—

Ron Driscoll 1987.

A. B. ("BANJO") PATERSON

Clancy of the Overflow

I had written him a letter which I had, for want of better
Knowledge, sent to where I met him down the Lachlan,
years ago;
He was shearing when I knew him, so I sent the letter to him,
Just on spec, addressed as follows, "Clancy, of The Overflow."

And an answer came directed in a writing unexpected
(And I think the same was written with a thumbnail dipped
in tar);
'Twas his shearing mate who wrote it, and *verbatim* I will
quote it:
"Clancy's gone to Queensland droving, and we don't know
where he are."

. . . . .

In my wild erratic fancy visions come to me of Clancy
Gone a-drovin "down the Cooper" where the Western
drovers go;
As the stock are slowly stringing, Clancy rides behind them
singing,
For the drover's life has pleasures that the townsfolk never
know.

And the bush has friends to meet him, and their kindly
voices greet him
In the murmur of the breezes and the river on its bars,
And he sees the vision splendid of the sunlit plains extended,
And at night the wondrous glory of the everlasting stars.

. . . . .

I am sitting in my dingy little office, where a stingy
Ray of sunlight struggles feebly down between the houses tall,
And the foetid air and gritty of the dusty, dirty city,
Through the open window floating, spreads its foulness over all.

Ron Driscoll
1987

And in place of lowing cattle, I can hear the fiendish rattle
Of the tramways and the 'buses making hurry down the street;
And the language uninviting of the gutter children fighting
Comes fitfully and faintly through the ceaseless tramp of feet.

And the hurrying people daunt me, and their pallid faces haunt me
As they shoulder one another in their rush and nervous haste,
With their eager eyes and greedy, and their stunted forms and weedy,
For townsfolk have no time to grow, they have no time to waste.

And I somehow rather fancy that I'd like to change with Clancy,
Like to take a turn at droving where the seasons come and go,
While he faced the round eternal of the cash-book and the journal—
But I doubt he'd suit the office, Clancy, of The Overflow.

—oOo—

Ron Driscoll 1987

JOHN SHAW NEILSON

The Crane Is My Neighbour

The bird is my neighbour, a whimsical fellow and dim;
There is in the lake a nobility falling on him.

The bird is a noble, he turns to the sky for a theme,
And the ripples are thoughts coming out to the edge of a
dream.

The bird is both ancient and excellent, sober and wise,
But he never could spend all the love that is sent for his eyes.

He bleats no instruction, he is not an arrogant drummer;
His gown is simplicity—blue as the smoke of the summer.

How patient he is as he puts out his wings for the blue!
His eyes are as old as the twilight, and calm as the dew.

The bird is my neighbour, he leaves not a claim for a sigh,
He moves as the guest of the sunlight—he roams in the sky.

The bird is a noble, he turns to the sky for a theme,
And the ripples are thoughts coming out to the edge of a
dream.

—oOo—

Ron Driscoll
1987

CHARLES HARPUR

A Midsummer Noon in the Australian Forest

Not a sound disturbs the air,
There is quiet everywhere;
Over plains and over woods
What a mighty stillness broods!

All the birds and insects keep
Where the coolest shadows sleep;
Even the busy ants are found
Resting in their pebbled mound;
Even the locust clingeth now
Silent to the barky bough:
Over hills and over plains
Quiet, vast and slumbrous, reigns.

Only there's a drowsy humming
From yon warm lagoon slow coming:
'Tis the dragon-hornet—see!
All bedaubed resplendently,
Yellow on a tawny ground—
Each rich spot nor square nor round,
Rudely heart-shaped, as it were

The blurred and hasty impress there
Of a vermeil-crusted seal
Dusted o'er with golden meal.
Only there's a droning where
Yon bright beetle shines in air,
Tracks it in its gleaming flight
With a slanting beam of light,
Rising in the sunshine higher,
Till its shards flame out like fire.

RonDriscoll
1987

CHARLES HARPUR

Every other thing is still,
Save the ever-wakeful rill,
Whose cool murmur only throws
Cooler comfort round repose;
Or some ripple in the sea
Of leafy boughs, where, lazily,
Tired summer, in her bower
Turning with the noontide hour,
Heaves a slumbrous breath ere she
Once more slumbers peacefully.

O 'tis easeful here to lie
Hidden from noon's scorching eye,
In this grassy cool recess
Musing thus of quietness.

—o○o—

Ron Driscoll
1987

JAMES DEVANEY

The Willows

Dawn, and the stars yet there,
Like revellers overstayed,
And I watch the shadowy twilight
Vaguely the dark invade;
I see slowly emerging
The river willow-lined,
And a strange winter daybreak
Looms the hill behind.

The kingfisher head-heavy
His first patrol has tried
Along the falling willows
That love the river-side.
You poets city-weary,
I'll tell you a lovely thing:
Shadows of trees on water
At the day's first wakening.

The misty breath of morning
Like a cool hand on the brow,
And skies begin to opal,
And day is here now.
Poets, I know a poem
That never shall be old:
Willows along a water,
And their green hair going gold.

—oOo—

Ron Driscoll
1987

BARCROFT BOAKE

Where the Dead Men Lie

Out on the wastes of the Never Never—
That's where the dead men lie!
There where the heat-waves dance for ever—
That's where the dead men lie!
That's where the Earth's loved sons are keeping
Endless tryst: not the west wind sweeping
Feverish pinions can wake their sleeping—
Out where the dead men lie!

Where brown Summer and Death have mated—
That's where the dead men lie!
Loving with fiery lust unsated—
That's where the dead men lie!
Out where the grinning skulls bleach whitely
Under the saltbush sparkling brightly;
Out where the wild dogs chorus nightly—
That's where the dead men lie!

Deep in the yellow, flowing river—
That's where the dead men lie!
Under the banks where the shadows quiver—
That's where the dead men lie!
Where the platypus twists and doubles,
Leaving a train of tiny bubbles;
Rid at last of their earthly troubles—
That's where the dead men lie!

East and backward pale faces turning—
That's how the dead men lie!
Gaunt arms stretched with a voiceless yearning—
That's how the dead men lie!
Oft in the fragrant hush of nooning
Hearing again their mother's crooning,
Wrapt for aye in a dreamful swooning—
That's how the dead men lie!

Ron Driscoll 1989.

Only the hand of Night can free them—
  That's when the dead men fly!
Only the frightened cattle see them—
  See the dead men go by!
Cloven hoofs beating out one measure,
Bidding the stockmen know no leisure—
That's when the dead men take their pleasure!
  That's when the dead men fly!

Ask, too, the never-sleeping drover:
  He sees the dead pass by;
Hearing them call to their friends—the plover,
  Hearing the dead men cry;
Seeing their faces stealing, stealing,
Hearing their laughter, pealing, pealing,
Watching their grey forms wheeling, wheeling
  Round where the cattle lie!

Strangled by thirst and fierce privation—
  That's how the dead men die!
Out on Moneygrub's farthest station—
  That's how the dead men die!
Hard-faced greybeards, youngsters callow;
Some mounds cared for, some left fallow;
Some deep down, yet others shallow;
  Some having but the sky.

Moneygrub, as he sips his claret,
  Looks with complacent eye
Down at his watch-chain, eighteen carat—
  There, in his club, hard by:
Recks not that every link is stamped with
Names of the men whose limbs are cramped with
Too long lying in grave-mould, cramped with
  Death where the dead men lie.

Ron Driscoll
1987

Ballad of the Drover

Across the stony ridges,
Across the rolling plain,
Young Harry Dale, the drover,
Comes riding home again.
And well his stock-horse bears him,
And light of heart is he,
And stoutly his old packhorse
Is trotting by his knee.

Up Queensland way with cattle
He's travelled regions vast,
And many months have vanished
Since home-folks saw him last.
He hums a song of someone
He hopes to marry soon;
And hobble-chains and camp-ware
Keep jingling to the tune.

Beyond the hazy dado
Against the lower skies
And yon blue line of ranges
The station homestead lies.
And thitherward the drover
Jogs through the lazy noon,
While hobble-chains and camp-ware
Are jingling to a tune.

An hour has filled the heavens
With storm-clouds inky black;
At times the lightning trickles
Around the drover's track;
But Harry pushes onward,
His horses' strength he tries,
In hope to reach the river
Before the flood shall rise.

The thunder, pealing o'er him,
Goes rumbling down the plain;
And sweet on thirsty pastures
Beats fast the plashing rain;
Then every creek and gully
Sends forth its tribute flood—
The river runs a banker,
All stained with yellow mud.

Now Harry speaks to Rover,
The best dog on the plains,
And to his hardy horses,
And strokes their shaggy manes:
"We've breasted bigger rivers
When floods were at their height,
Nor shall this gutter stop us
From getting home tonight!"

The thunder growls a warning,
The blue, forked lightnings gleam;
The drover turns his horses
To swim the fatal stream.
But, oh! the flood runs stronger
Than e'er it ran before;
The saddle-horse is failing,
And only half-way o'er!

When flashes next the lightning
The flood's grey breast is blank;
A cattle-dog and packhorse
Are struggling up the bank.
But in the lonely homestead
The girl shall wait in vain—
He'll never pass the stations
In charge of stock again.

Ron Driscoll
1987

The faithful dog a moment
Lies panting on the bank,
Then plunges through the current
To where his master sank.
And round and round in circles
He fights with failing strength,
Till, gripped by wilder waters,
He fails and sinks at length.

Across the flooded lowlands
And slopes of sodden loam
The packhorse struggles bravely
To take dumb tidings home;
And mud-stained, wet, and weary,
He goes by rock and tree,
With clanging chains and tinware
All sounding eerily.

—oOo—

Ron Driscoll
1987

MARY HANNAY FOOTT

Where the Pelican Builds

The horses were ready, the rails were down,
But the riders lingered still—
One had a parting word to say,
And one had his pipe to fill.
Then they mounted, one with a granted prayer,
And one with a grief unguessed.
"We are going," they said as they rode away,
"Where the pelican builds her nest!"

They had told us of pastures wide and green,
To be sought past the sunset's glow;
Of rifts in the ranges by opal lit;
And gold 'neath the river's flow.
And thirst and hunger were banished words
When they spoke of that unknown West;
No drought they dreaded, no flood they feared,
Where the pelican builds her nest!

The creek at the ford was but fetlock deep
When we watched them crossing there;
The rains have replenished it thrice since then,
And thrice has the rock lain bare.
But the waters of Hope have flowed and fled,
And never from blue hill's breast
Come back—by the sun and the sands devoured—
Where the pelican builds her nest.

—oOo—

Ron Driscoll 1987

HENRY LAWSON

The Song and the Sigh

The creek went down with a broken song,
  'Neath the sheoaks high;
The waters carried the song along,
  And the oaks a sigh.

The song and the sigh went winding by,
  Went winding down;
Circling the foot of the mountain high,
  And the hillside brown.

They were hushed in the swamp of the Dead Man's Crime,
  Where the curlews cried;
But they reached the river the self-same time,
  And there they died.

And the creek of life goes winding on,
  Wandering by;
And bears for ever, its course upon
  A song and a sigh.

—oOo—

Ron Driscoll
1987

MARY GILMORE

From *Swans at Night*

Within the night, above the dark,
I heard a host upon the air,
Upon the void they made no mark,
For all that they went sailing there.

And from that host there came a cry,
A note of calling strange and high;
I heard it blown against the sky,
Till naught there seemed but it and I.

A long and lonely wraith of sound,
It floated out in distance wide,
As though it knew another bound,
A space wherein it never died.

I heard the swans, I heard the swans,
I heard the swans that speed by night;
That ever, where the starlight wans,
Fly on unseen within the height.

I never knew how wide the dark,
I never knew the depth of space,
I never knew how frail a bark,
How small is man within his place,

Not till I heard the swans go by,
Not till I marked their haunting cry,
Not till, within the vague on high,
I watched them pass across the sky.

. . . . .

I never knew how vast the sky,
I never knew how small was I,
Until I heard, remote and high,
The distant swans' far floated cry.

Ron Driscoll
1987

HENRY LAWSON

To a Pair of Blucher Boots

Old acquaintance unforgotten,
  Tho' you may be "ugly brutes"—
Tho' your leather's cracked and rotten,
  Worn-out pair of Blucher boots.

'Tis the richer man before you,
  Dearer leathers grace his feet;
'Twas the better man that wore you
  In the tramps thro' dust and heat!

Oft rebuffed by "super's" snarling,
  When I asked him for a "show",
On that long tramp to the Darling
  In the days of long ago;

Tell me, if you know it, whether,
  As I sadly tramped away,
Bore I heavy on your leather,
  Worn-out pair of Bluchers, say?

Tho' your leather's cracked and rotten,
  Tho' you may be ugly brutes,
I'll preserve you unforgotten,
  Worn-out pair of Blucher boots!

—oOo—

Ron Driscoll
1987

JOHN O'BRIEN

Calling To Me

Through the hush of my heart in the spell of its dreaming
  Comes the song of a bush boy glad-hearted and free;
Oh, the gullies are green where the sunlight is streaming,
  And the voice of that youngster is calling to me.

It is calling to me with a haunting insistence,
  And my feet wander off on a hoof-beaten track,
Till I hear the old magpies away in the distance
  With a song of the morning that's calling me back.

It is calling me back, for the dew's on the clover,
  And the colours are mellow on mountain and tree;
Oh, the gold has gone gray in the heart of the rover,
  And the bush in the sunshine is calling to me.

It is calling to me, though the breezes are telling
  Gay troubadour tales to the stars as they roam;
For the tapers are lit in the humble old dwelling,
  And the love that it sheltered is calling me home.

It is calling me home—but the white road lies gleaming,
  And afar from it all must I tarry and dree;
Just an echo far off, in the hush of my dreaming,
  Is the voice of a youngster that's calling to me.

—oOo—

Ron Driscoll
1987

C. J. DENNIS

West

"*I've* seen so much uv dirt an' grime
I'm mad to 'ave things clean.
I've seen so much uv death," 'e said—
"So many cobbers lyin' dead—
You won't know wot I mean;
But, lad, I've 'ad so much uv strife
I want things straightened in my life.

"I've seen so much uv 'ate," 'e said—
"Mad 'ate an' silly rage—
I'm yearnin' for clear thoughts," said 'e.
"Kindness an' love seem good to me.
I want a new, white page
To start all over, clean an' good,
An' live me life as reel men should."

We're sittin' talkin' by the fence,
The sun's jist goin' down,
Paintin' the sky all gold an' pink.
Said 'e. "When it's like that, I think—"
An' then 'e stops to frown.
Said 'e, "I think, when it's jist so,
Uv … God or somethin': I dunno.

"I ain't seen much uv God," said 'e;
"Not 'ere nor Over There;
But, partly wot the padre said,
It gits me when I stare
Out West when it's like that is now.
There must be somethin' else—some'ow

RonDriscoll
1987.

"I've thought a lot," said Digger Smith—
  "Out There I thought a lot.
I thought uv death, an' all the rest,
An' uv me mates, good mates gone West;
  An' it ain't much I've got;
But things get movin' in me 'ead
When I look over there," 'e said.

"I've seen so much uv death," said 'e,
  "Me mind is in a whirl.
I've 'ad so many thoughts uv late." ...
Said I, "Now, tell me, tell me straight,
  Own up; ain't there a girl?"
Said 'e, "I've done the best I can.
Wot does she want with 'arf a man?"

It weren't no use. 'E wouldn't talk
  Uv nothin' but the sky.
Said 'e. "Now, dinkum, talkin' square,
When you git gazin' over there
  Don't you 'arf want to cry?
I wouldn't be su'prised to see
An angel comin' out," said 'e.

The gold was creepin' up, the sun
  Was 'arf be'ind the range:
It don't seem strange a man should cry
To see that glory in the sky—
  To me it don't seem strange.
"Digger!" said 'e. "Look at it now!
There must be somethin' else—some'ow."

—oOo—